S0-BDO-379

CAVES

EARLY BIRD EARTH SCIENCE

BY SALLY M. WALKER

LERNER PUBLICATIONS COMPANY • MINNEAPOLIS

The photographs in this book are used with the permission of: NPS Photo by Peter Jones, pp. 1, 1 (title type), 5, 6 (background), 10 (background), 20 (background), 24, 25, 28 (background), 34 (background), 36, 44–47 (backgrounds), 48 (top); © James May/SuperStock, p. 4; © Prisma/SuperStock, pp. 6, 16; © Hubert Stadler/CORBIS, p. 7; © Robert Dowling/CORBIS, p. 8; NPS Photo by Gary Berdeaux, p. 9; NPS Photo by Keir Morse, p. 10; © Marc Muench/CORBIS, p. 12; © Peter Lane Taylor/Visuals Unlimited, p. 14; © Jon Arnold Images/SuperStock, p. 15; © Peter Essick/Aurora/Getty Images, p. 17; © Isu/Stock4B/Getty Images, p. 18; © blickwinkel/Alamy, p. 20; © Stephen Alvarez/Time Life Pictures/Getty Images, p. 21; Ronal C. Kerbo, p. 22; © Tom & Susan Bean/Stone/Getty Images, p. 23; © Richard Thom/Visuals Unlimited, pp. 26, 31; © Getty Images, p. 27; © Kjell B. Sandved/Visuals Unlimited, p. 28; © Tom Brakefield/SuperStock, p. 29; NPS Photo, pp. 30, 35, 48 (bottom); © Daniel W. Gotshall/Visuals Unlimited, p. 32; © Stephen L. Alvarez/National Geographic/Getty Images, p. 33; © age fotostock/SuperStock, pp. 34, 46; © Annette Summers Engel, pp. 37, 39; © Ladi Kirn/Alamy, p. 38; © Scott A. Engel, p. 40; © Dave Bunnell, p. 41; © Chris Howes/Wild Places Photography/Alamy, p. 42; © Danny Lehman/CORBIS, p. 43; © AM Corporation/Alamy, p. 47.

Front cover: © Hubert Stadler/CORBIS
Front cover title type: NPS Photo by Peter Jones
Back cover: © Reuters/CORBIS

Illustrations on pp. 11, 13, 19 by © Laura Westlund/Independent Picture Service

Lerner Publications Company
A division of Lerner Publishing Group, Inc.
241 First Avenue North
Minneapolis, MN 55401 U.S.A.

Website address: www.lernerbooks.com

Library of Congress Cataloging-in-Publication Data

Walker, Sally M.
Caves / by Sally M. Walker.
p. cm. — (Early bird earth science)
Includes index.
ISBN-13: 978-0-8225-6734-9 (lib. bdg. : alk. paper)
1. Caves—Juvenile literature. 2. Cave ecology—Juvenile literature. I. Title.
GB601.2.W35 2008
551.44'7—dc22 2006038098

Manufactured in the United States of America
1 2 3 4 5 6 - JR - 13 12 11 10 09 08

CONTENTS

BE A WORD DETECTIVE

Can you find these words as you read about caves? Be a detective and try to figure out what they mean. You can turn to the glossary on page 46 for help.

bedrock
calcite
cavern
dissolve
echoes
formations
groundwater
limestone
minerals
sinkhole
stalactites
stalagmite

This underground room is a cave. It is on the island of Barbados in the Caribbean Sea. Where else in the world are caves?

CHAPTER 1

WHAT IS A CAVE?

Imagine a place that is dark and cool. The icy air chills your body on a hot summer day. A river flows out of rock. Stone icicles drip water. A group of bats suddenly appears. All of these things can happen in a cave.

A cave is an underground hole. It has an opening onto Earth's surface. Many caves are large enough for a person to go inside.

Almost every country in the world has caves. Most caves are small. And most types of caves take a very long time to form.

Some caves are filled with water.

Caves may have many chambers. A chamber is like a room. The largest chamber ever discovered is Sarawak Chamber. It is in Gunung Mulu National Park in the country of Malaysia.

Sarawak Chamber is 2,300 feet long and 1,480 feet wide at its widest point. The ceiling of the chamber is 230 feet high.

Mammoth Cave has more than 350 miles of underground passages and chambers. To reach the Drapery Room, you have to go down 49 stairs.

A large cave is called a cavern. A cavern often has more than one chamber. Tunnels connect the chambers. Mammoth Cave is a cavern in the state of Kentucky. Most parts of Mammoth Cave are far from an outside opening. Many of the cave's chambers are lit up with electric lights. Without the lights, it would be too dark inside to see.

This cave formed when huge rocks broke off from a mountain and tumbled down to this spot. What is this kind of cave called?

CHAPTER 2

KINDS OF CAVES

One cave can be very different from another. That's because caves form in different ways. One kind of cave forms from broken chunks of bedrock. Bedrock is a thick layer of solid rock under the soil. Sometimes water and wind wear away the soil. Then you can see the bedrock.

Stones and big boulders (BOHL-derz) are rocks that have broken off from bedrock. Sometimes boulders, small rocks, and soil slide down a mountain. They land in a pile at the bottom. The boulders lean against one another. Water from rain or a stream washes away the soil and small rocks. A space is left under the boulders. The space is called a talus (TA-luhs) cave.

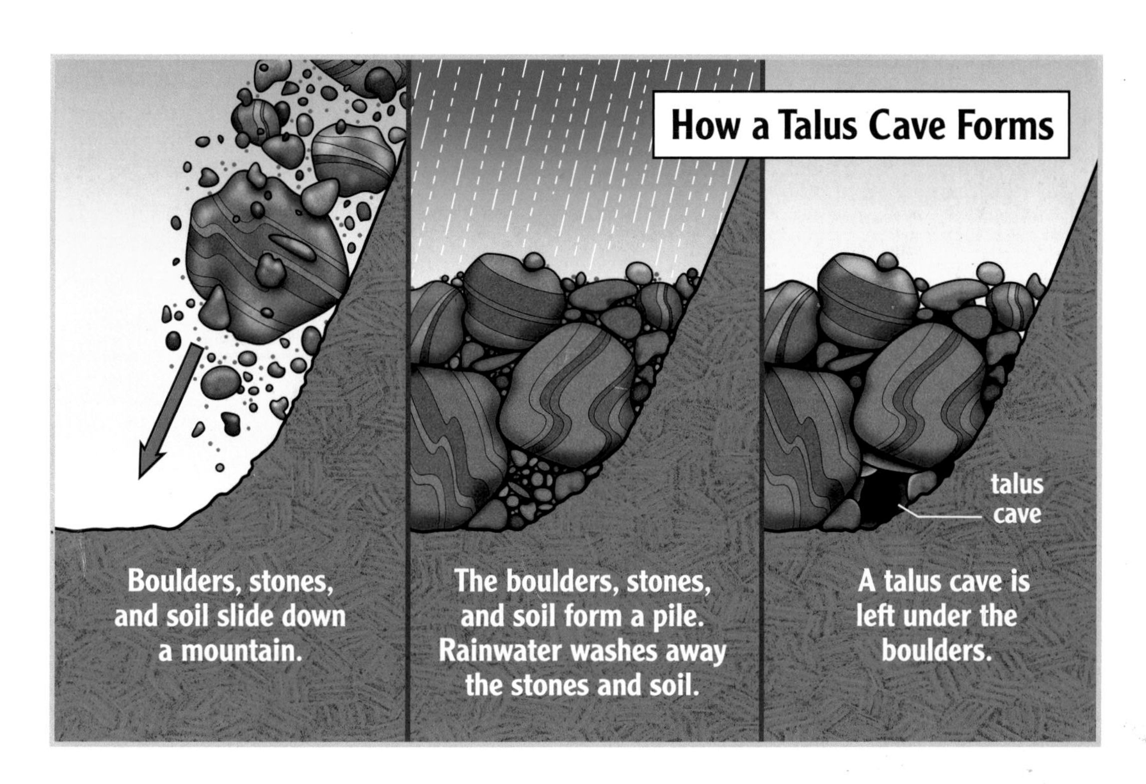

Melted rock deep inside Earth can make another kind of cave. Melted rock flows out of volcanoes when they erupt. When the liquid rock is on Earth's surface, it is called lava. Streams of thick lava flow away from a volcano. The surface of the flowing lava cools quickly. As it cools, a crust of solid rock forms.

This cave is the Thurston Lava Tube in Hawaii. Its floor, ceiling, and walls are made of lava that cooled and hardened.

Melted lava still flows beneath the crust, like liquid inside a drinking straw. Finally, lava stops flowing from the volcano. Lava beneath the hard crust drains away. An empty tube is left. The tube is a type of cave called a lava tube.

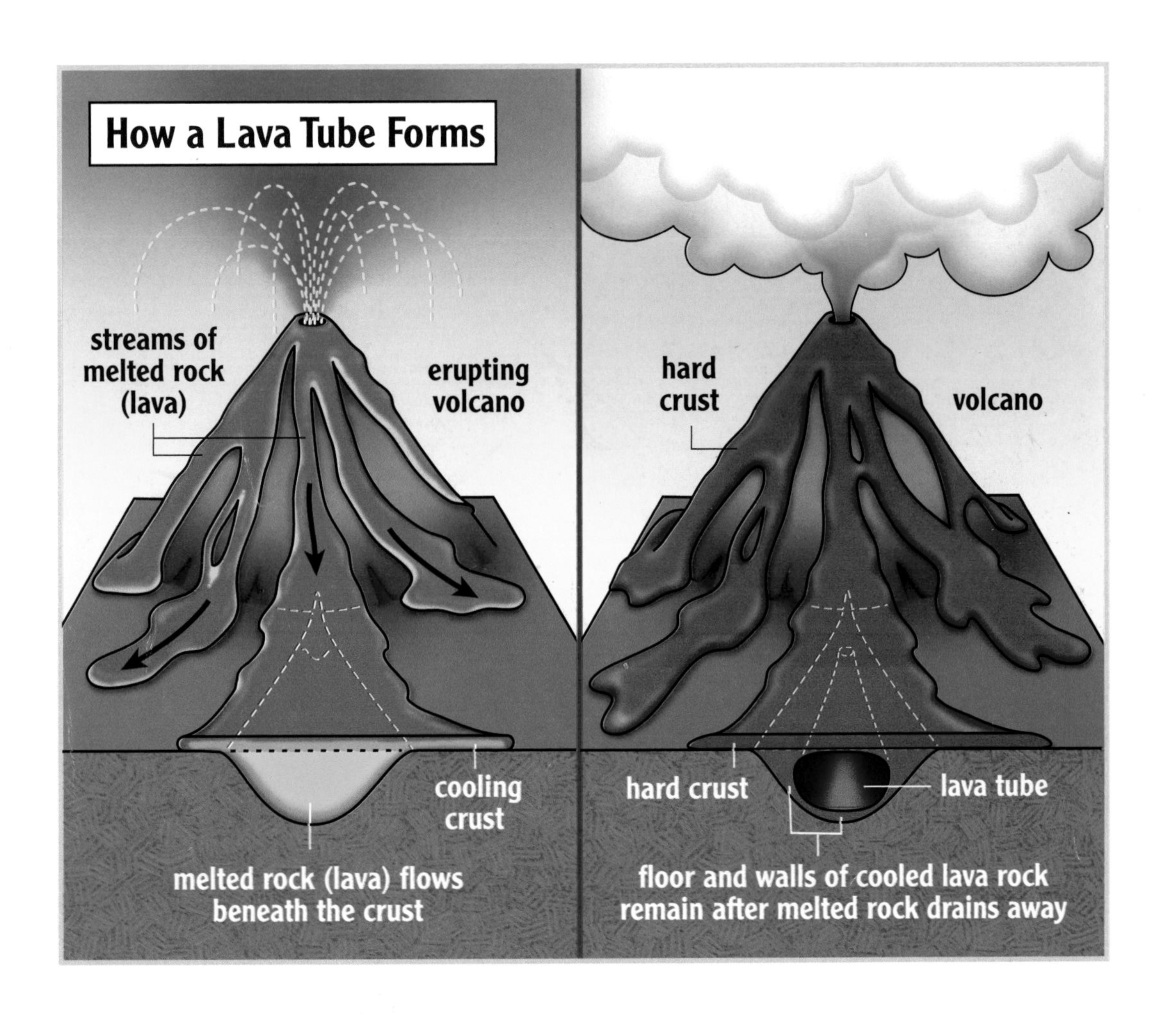

An icy river flows through a glacier (GLAY-shur) in Switzerland. These people are preparing to explore the river and the cave it flows through. Then they will make a map of the cave.

Caves also can form inside ice. A glacier is a large body of ice that moves slowly across land. It is so thick that it doesn't melt away in the summer. Sometimes part of the ice inside a glacier melts into water.

The water drains out of the glacier. As the water moves, it makes tunnels and caves in the ice. The caves are called glacier caves. The walls and ceiling of a glacier cave are made of ice.

Tourists can visit this glacier cave in France.

Water creates most other kinds of caves. In some places, bedrock cliffs are near the seashore. Ocean waves crash against the rock. Seawater flows into cracks in the cliffs. The water weakens the rock. Swirling water breaks off pieces of bedrock. Over time, the cracks get wider. They become holes. Holes made by ocean waves are called sea caves.

This photo was taken from inside a sea cave.

Usually, water inside the ground flows in tiny trickles. But at Thousand Springs in Idaho, water gushes out of holes and cracks in the bedrock.

Water also creates caves in bedrock that is underground. Soil and some kinds of rocks have tiny air spaces in them. And bedrock has cracks. Water flows through those air spaces and cracks. Water that flows inside the ground is called groundwater.

If you stir a small amount of sugar into liquid, the sugar will seem to disappear. It becomes part of the liquid. Bits of bedrock can disappear in the same way when groundwater flows through cracks in the rock.

Groundwater can make a cave. In some places, bedrock is made of limestone. Limestone is a type of rock. Groundwater can slowly make limestone dissolve (dih-ZAHLV). When something dissolves, it breaks up into tiny pieces and disappears.

Bits of limestone bedrock dissolve when groundwater flows through cracks in the bedrock. The cracks get bigger. Then more groundwater fills the cracks. It causes even more of the limestone to dissolve. After many years, the crack becomes a cave.

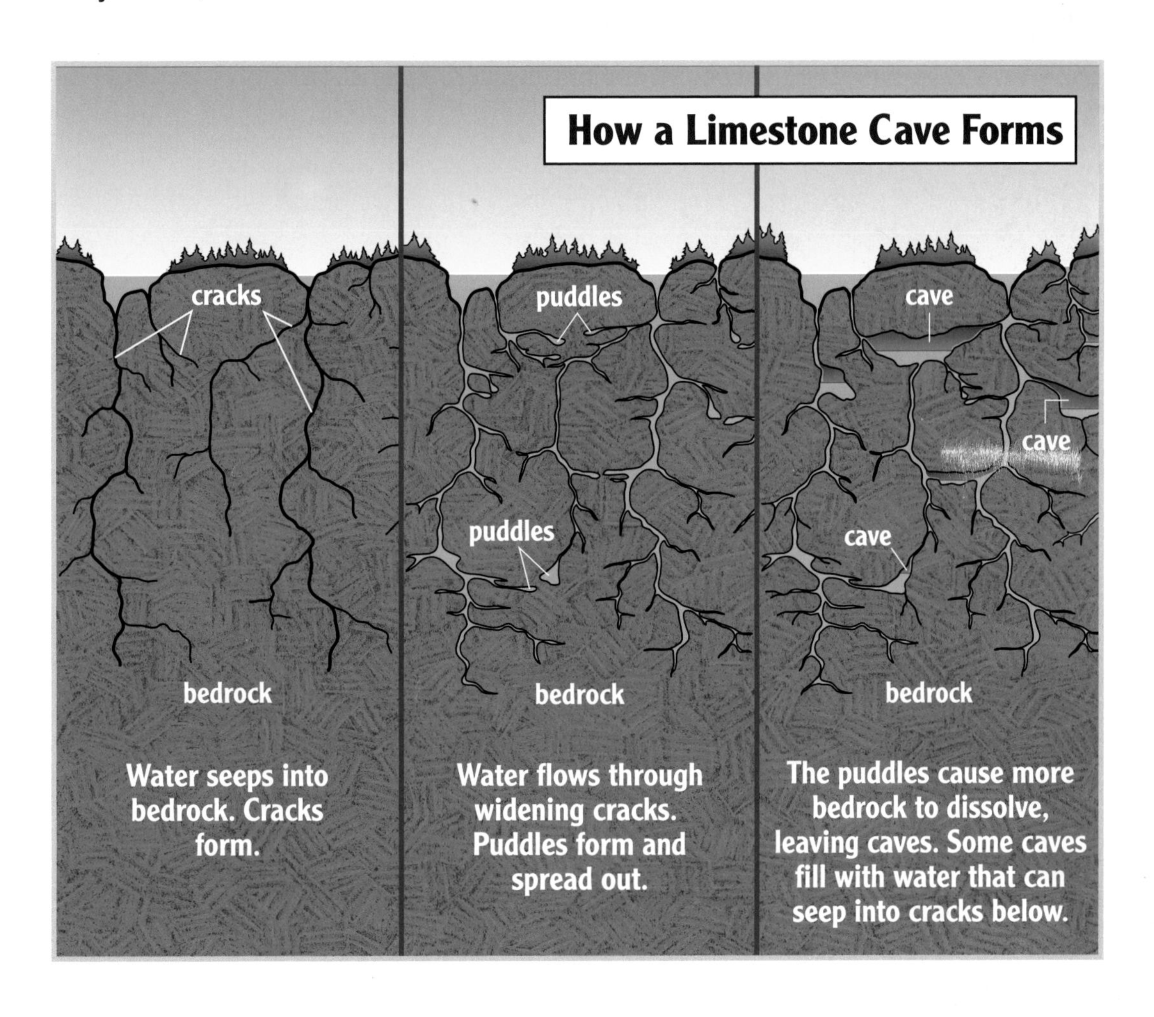

The long, skinny ceiling decorations in this cave are called soda straws. They are made by groundwater. How does groundwater make cave decorations?

CHAPTER 3

STONE ICICLES

After a long time, the groundwater that makes a limestone cave drains away. But some groundwater still seeps into the cave. It trickles along the ceiling and walls. Trickling groundwater creates formations inside the cave. Formations are shapes made out of rock.

Groundwater has natural chemicals in it. The chemicals combine and make minerals. A mineral is a solid, nonliving substance found in nature. Rocks are made of minerals. Minerals made from the chemicals in groundwater can pile up. The minerals can make amazing formations inside a cave.

Some formations are made as groundwater evaporates. When something evaporates, it changes from a liquid to a gas. This formation is called a gypsum (JIHP-suhm) flower. It formed as water evaporated and left behind the mineral gypsum.

Most cave formations are made of a mineral called calcite (KAL-site). Calcite is made from groundwater that has dissolved limestone in it. Calcite forms as the water meets air inside a cave. A chemical from the groundwater escapes into the air. Then the water can't hold as much dissolved limestone. So it leaves some behind as solid calcite.

This type of calcite formation is called flowstone. It is made by groundwater that is freely flowing instead of just dripping or trickling.

Water drips from the ends of small formations. The formations collect new calcite from each water drop.

Bits of calcite form on a cave's rocky ceiling, floor, and walls. More groundwater trickles into the cave. Each drop of groundwater that drips away leaves new calcite on top of the calcite that is already there. Drop by drop, a calcite formation is made.

Stalactites (stuh-LAK-tites) are calcite formations that hang from the ceiling of a cave. They look like stone icicles. Another kind of formation is called a stalagmite (stuh-LAG-mite). Stalagmites grow on a cave's floor. A stalagmite is like an icicle that points upward.

The tallest of these stalagmites is called the Totem Pole. It is in Carlsbad Caverns.

Columns reach from the ceiling to the floor. These columns are in the Doll's Theater, a chamber in Carlsbad Caverns.

Sometimes a stalactite forms right above a stalagmite. If they grow big enough, they meet in the middle. Joined together, the stalactite and the stalagmite become a column (KAH-luhm).

Can you see why this formation is called cave popcorn?

Not all calcite formations look like icicles. Some look like wavy curtains. Others look like flowers or popcorn. Some formations even look like fried eggs!

Most cave formations take thousands of years to form. But changes in a cave can also happen suddenly. A cave's bedrock ceiling may have cracks. Cracks weaken the ceiling. Sometimes it collapses. The bedrock above the cave crashes down. That makes a big hole in the ground. The hole is called a sinkhole.

Part of this road collapsed into a hole in the ground below it. People can get hurt if the ground below roads or buildings collapses. It's important to know where caves are. Then people can avoid building on top of a weak cave ceiling.

The lights on this cave ceiling are actually glowworms. Glowworms are often found in caves. What other animals live in caves?

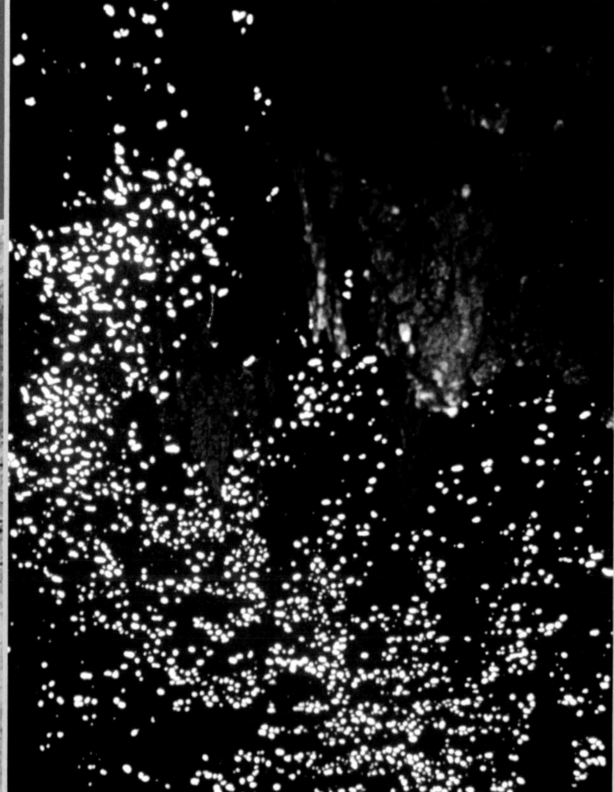

CHAPTER 4
ANIMAL LIFE

Many animals, such as bats, bears, and fish, live in caves. Snails, glowworms, spiders, and insects live in caves too. Caves also have tiny living things called bacteria (bak-TEER-ee-uh). Deep caves have bacteria that are not found anywhere else on Earth.

Some animals, such as bats and foxes, go in and out of caves. Others live their whole lives inside. Cave spiders, cave shrimp, and other cave animals live in total darkness. Their bodies are built to live in a dark place.

Foxes often rest or take shelter in small caves.

Most animals can see because light hits their eyes. But caves often have no light. Eyes cannot see inside a totally dark cave. So cave animals use other senses instead of sight. Some cave fish don't even have eyes.

This cave fish has no eyes. It feels its way around by using special body parts that are extrasensitive to movement in the water.

The bristly cave crayfish lives in caves in Missouri.

Some cave animals also have no skin color. Crayfish that live in caves may be completely white. They look like small, white lobsters. Salamanders and fish in caves may also be white.

Bats sleep inside caves during the day. They hang from the ceiling and walls. They leave the cave at night to find food.

Some bats fly deep inside caves. They find their way by making high-pitched sounds. The sounds are so high that human ears can't hear them.

The sounds bounce off the cave walls and back to the bats' ears. The sounds that bounce back are called echoes (EH-kohz). Echoes tell bats how close they are to the cave walls.

If you yelled inside a cave, your voice might echo off the walls. When bats fly inside a dark cave, they listen to their own echoes to find their way.

These people are visiting a cave in Mexico. How can caves be made safe for visitors?

CHAPTER 5

EXPLORING A CAVE

Caves are dangerous places. They are cold and damp. Cave floors are often slippery and may have deep cracks. Cave ceilings can collapse. But caves are beautiful too. And they can help people learn about Earth. So people still like to visit caves.

Parts of some large caverns have been made safe for people to visit. They have walkways, steps, and guardrails. These caves also have lights so people can see. Guides teach people about the cave and its formations. The guides have been trained to safely lead visitors through the caves.

Large staircases lead tourists down into Mammoth Cave. The man wearing a hat is a guide at Mammoth Cave National Park.

People explore caves for many reasons. Some scientists want to learn more about animals that live in caves. Others study cave formations to find out about Earth's past. Cave formations have been growing for thousands of years. So they contain clues about what Earth's air and water were like long ago.

Devil's Spring is part of Carlsbad Caverns. Its formations have grown layer by layer over many years.

These scientists are testing the water of a cave stream in Wyoming.

Some scientists study the groundwater inside caves. A lot of the water we drink comes from groundwater. People can get sick if they drink water that has harmful substances in it. So scientists try to find out what substances are in the groundwater. Then they know if the water is safe for people to drink.

Cave explorers practice a cave rescue. They need to know how to safely help someone in an emergency.

Some people explore caves as an adventure. But these people and scientists all follow rules. The rules help to keep them safe.

Cavers never go caving alone. They go with at least two other adults who have been caving before. If someone gets hurt, one person can go get help while another stays with the injured person.

Cavers take several sources of light with them, such as a flashlight and a candle and matches. Then if the flashlight batteries die, the cavers will still have a way to see. And before they go, cavers tell someone what cave they will be visiting and when they will be back. Then if an emergency happens in the cave, someone will be able to send help.

Most cavers wear headlights on their helmets. Then they can use their hands for moving through a cave instead of holding a flashlight.

Finally, cavers must have the right equipment. Experienced cavers often explore caves that are deep underground. They use special ropes and other equipment to get down into these caves. They know how to fasten the ropes properly so no one will fall and get hurt.

This caver is wearing a helmet, a headlight, gloves, and kneepads. A system of special straps called a harness fits around her body. The harness keeps her safely attached to the rope.

This cave has been damaged by careless visitors who wrote on the walls.

People also follow rules to protect caves. Caves are easily damaged. It takes nature many thousands of years to make a large cave. But a thoughtless caver can ruin it in a few minutes.

Careful cavers follow the "leave no trace" rules. That means they don't do anything in a cave that would show that they had been there.

If you visit a cave, you can be a careful caver too. Never break off part of a formation. Try not to even touch the cave walls or formations. Your hands have germs and oils. The germs might harm the cave animals. The oils on your skin could harm the formations. Don't litter or leave food crumbs inside a cave. Leave the cave looking the same way it did when you entered. That way, other people can enjoy it too.

Tourists have broken off these stalactites in Cango Cave in the country of South Africa.

Nature is always shaping and changing caves. As long as visitors are careful not to damage caves or formations, many other people will be able to visit and enjoy caves in the future.

Caves are some of Earth's treasures. They are dark and mysterious. They are places where you can learn about nature. They are places of amazing beauty.

Almost every state and country has caves. Ask an adult to help you find out where the closest cave is. What secrets can your cave teach you?

A NOTE TO ADULTS
ON SHARING A BOOK

When you share a book with a child, you show that reading is important. To get the most out of the experience, read in a comfortable, quiet place. Turn off the television and limit other distractions, such as telephone calls. Be prepared to start slowly. Take turns reading parts of this book. Stop occasionally and discuss what you're reading. Talk about the photographs. If the child begins to lose interest, stop reading. When you pick up the book again, revisit the parts you have already read.

BE A VOCABULARY DETECTIVE

The word list on page 5 contains words that are important in understanding the topic of this book. Be word detectives and search for the words as you read the book together. Talk about what the words mean and how they are used in the sentence. Do any of these words have more than one meaning? You will find the words defined in a glossary on page 46.

WHAT ABOUT QUESTIONS?

Use questions to make sure the child understands the information in this book. Here are some suggestions:

> What did this paragraph tell us? What does this picture show? What do you think we'll learn about next? What is one way that water can make a cave? How do stalagmites and stalactites form? What can visitors do to protect caves? What is your favorite part of the book? Why?

If the child has questions, don't hesitate to respond with questions of your own, such as: What do *you* think? Why? What is it that you don't know? If the child can't remember certain facts, turn to the index.

INTRODUCING THE INDEX

The index helps readers find information without searching through the whole book. Turn to the index on page 48. Choose an entry such as *limestone* and ask the child to use the index to find out how a cave forms in limestone. Repeat with as many entries as you like. Ask the child to point out the differences between an index and a glossary. (The index helps readers find information, while the glossary tells readers what words mean.)

LEARN MORE ABOUT
CAVES

BOOKS

Brimner, Larry Dane. *Caves.* New York: Children's Press, 2000.

Gaff, Jackie. *I Wonder Why Stalactites Hang Down and Other Questions about Caves.* Boston: Kingfisher, 2003.

Petersen, David. *Carlsbad Caverns National Park.* Chicago: Children's Press, 1994.

Riley, Joelle. *Erosion.* Minneapolis: Lerner Publications Company, 2007.

Warner, Gertrude Chandler. *The Mystery in the Cave.* Morton Grove, IL: A. Whitman, 1996.

WEBSITES

DragonflyTV: Caves by Marie and Michelle
http://pbskids.org/dragonflytv/show/caves.html
Watch a video of young explorers Marie and Michelle as they travel inside a cave to study the formations. You can also read about what they discovered.

Exploring Caves
http://interactive2.usgs.gov/learningweb/teachers/explorecaves_explore.htm
Learn more about cave types, cave animals, and how to care for caves. This website, created by the U.S. Geological Survey, also shows where caves are in the United States.

GLOSSARY

bedrock: a thick layer of solid rock under soil, water, and loose rocks on Earth's surface

calcite (KAL-site): a mineral that makes up some cave formations

cavern: a large cave

dissolve (dih-ZAHLV): break up into tiny pieces and disappear in liquid

echoes (EH-kohz): sounds that bounce off a surface and back toward their maker

formations: shapes made out of rock

groundwater: water inside the ground

limestone: a type of rock that makes up some of the rock layer beneath Earth's surface

minerals: solid, nonliving substances found in nature

sinkhole: a hole in the ground that is made when a cave's ceiling falls down

stalactites (stuh-LAK-tites): formations that look like icicles hanging from the ceiling of a cave

stalagmite (stuh-LAG-mite): a formation that looks like an icicle sticking up from the floor of a cave

INDEX

Pages listed in **bold** type refer to photographs.